THE MISADVENTURES OF A NEW ENTREPRENEUR

5 Things They Won't Teach You In Business School

By:

Andrena Sawyer

Copyright © 2018 by Andrena Sawyer. All rights reserved.

No part of this publication may be reproduced, stored in a retrieval system, or transmitted in any form or by any means, electronic, mechanical, photocopying, recording, scanning, or otherwise, without the prior written permission of the author.

Limit of Liability/Disclaimer of Warranty: While the publisher and author have used their best efforts in preparing this book, they make no representations or warranties with respect to the accuracy or completeness of the contents of this book and specifically disclaim any implied warranties of merchantability or fitness for a particular purpose. No warranty may be created or extended by sales representatives or written sales materials. The advice and strategies contained herein may not be suitable for your situation. You should consult with a professional when appropriate. Neither the publisher nor the author shall be liable for any loss of profit or any other commercial damages, including but not limited to special, incidental, consequential, personal, or other damages.

DEDICATION

To those walking by faith, and not by sight.
Your commitment is not in vain.

TABLE OF CONTENTS

DEDICATION..

TABLE OF CONTENTS ....

INTRODUCTION ....

LESSON 1: THE WHOLE THING IS A BIG FAT LIE (MENTAL HEALTH)..............................

Business Tip #1: Building From Within — Infrastructure Is Everything! ....

LESSON 2: SORRY, I CAN'T HANG RIGHT NOW. I'M IN THE MIDDLE OF GRINDING (SOCIAL HEALTH) ....

Business Tip #2: Be S.M.A.R.T. ....

LESSON 3: SOMETIMES YOU JUST CAN'T FAKE IT UNTIL YOU MAKE IT (EMOTIONAL HEALTH) ....

Business Tip #3: Marry the Mission. Date the Model ....

LESSON 4: WHERE DID THOSE 30 LBS COME FROM? (PHYSICAL HEALTH) ....

Business Tip #4: Stick-to-it-ness — the Difference-maker...

LESSON 5: YOU MEAN IT WAS NEVER UP TO ME IN THE FIRST PLACE? (SPIRITUAL HEALTH)..

Business Tip #5: Cashflow Is King. Diversification Is His Queen.................................

BONUS: THE #TUESDAYTIP SERIES................

BUSINESS DEVELOPMENT TEMPLATES ....

ABOUT THE AUTHOR ....

OTHER BOOKS BY ANDRENA SAWYER ....
    Fiction ....
    Nonfiction ....

Introduction

So, you want to be an entrepreneur? There's bad news and good news. The bad news is that it may not be at all like what you see on social media — the serene photos on the beach, instafame, and the perfect work/life balance. The truth is, only a handful of people get to experience that consistently, and those who do pay their dues for an average of 15 years. But don't be discouraged! There's good news too, which is that freedom and autonomy are real, and so is the thrill of doing something that you love day in and day out. The question is: how do some people do it?

According to research from the Small Business Administration, only half of new businesses survive for the first five years, and only 35% are able to survive for 10 years. Even grimmer, Bloomberg research shows that 8 out of every 10 businesses fail within the first 19 months. Common reasons for business failure include leadership and management failure, weak value proposition, unprofitable business model, and poor financial management. Entrepreneur and business consultant Andrena Sawyer shares the secrets that every new entrepreneur should know. From the value of infrastructure to remaining relevant, aspiring and operational entrepreneurs will learn:

- How to build a sustainable business from within;
- How to create a healthy work/life balance;
- How to stay true to their original vision, while creating a model that consistently engages their audience; and
- Creating cashflow streams that will enable them to defy the odds and beat the statistics.

Lesson 1: The Whole Thing Is a Big Fat Lie (Mental Health)

I'm assuming you picked up this book because you're really serious about this entrepreneurship thing. You've watched other successful entrepreneurs live out their dreams of self-employment: flexible schedules, influential connections, and more money than they know what to do with, right? You want a piece of the pie too, not so? What if I told you that the first hurdle is simply surviving and keeping your doors open for the first few years, and that there are a few other hurdles after that, and you have to jump all of them without having a breakdown every other day? What if I told you it was all a big fat lie? Ok, so maybe not all of it, but there's a good lot of it that's not at all like what you see on Instagram or Shark Tank.

A common misconception is that if you quit

your job, follow your passion, and give it all you've got, you'll become an instant success. The truth is that most overnight successes are not successful overnight. After founding Microsoft in 1975, it took Bill Gates six years to land a contract with IBM to provide their base operating system. It then took another five years before Microsoft went public, therefore taking approximately 11 years to become an overnight success. Similarly, Apple was first established in 1976, but didn't really get on the map until the Macintosh was invented in 1984. Even then, it wasn't until the advent of the iMac and consumer products that the company started making strides toward becoming a household name. It took Steve Jobs nearly two decades to become an overnight success. Facebook is no exception to the not-so-overnight phenomenon. Founded in 2003 as "Facemash," Facebook still showed a yearly net loss of $3.63 million two years later. It was nearly five years later that the company began to be profitable. Whether you have the potential to become a multi-billion-dollar corporation, or your goal is to stay small and connected locally, the universal truth is that building your empire will take time.

It has taken me several years to begin to see

what others saw in my journey as successful. I'm not talking self-deprecation rooted in low self-esteem here. I'm talking about the paradox of what others see in you and what you see on the backend. See, while others saw a blossoming company from a courageous 20-something-year-old who quit her job and, in a relatively short time, had staff and an office working for herself, I was dealing with the reality of needing those staff, and going without a paycheck for several months so that I could afford to keep all the things that others were congratulating me on.

I remember the first time I had to talk with a staff member to explain to them that their paycheck would be late. I agonized for weeks. I'd done the best I could, sacrificed my own stability for the sake of the purpose, considered that they had bills and a family who depended on them, and there really was no other way to make the money just appear. Here I was, the leader—the one who was supposed to have all the solutions, and I was fresh out of ideas. I remember inviting that employee to sit with me in our conference room so we could talk. The power dynamics at play instantly made her feel like she was in trouble. I saw it in her eyes, and inside I shrunk at the fact that really, I was the one that was in trouble. The meeting started lightly, and I made a small joke, telling her to relax because I just needed to tell her something important. She did, but I didn't. Despite my best effort, I couldn't conquer the embarrassment, fear, anxiety, and uncertainty. I stopped beating around the bush long enough to apologize profusely and tell her that her paycheck was just going to be a few days late, at best.

The truth was that was wishful thinking. I could hope it would be a couple of days, but only if another new client signed a contract in the next day or two. However, according to my calculations, it could be as much as a couple of weeks. I couldn't, in good conscience, tell her that, knowing that she was a faithful employee who expected to get paid on time for the work that she was doing. I also couldn't tell her that, because if she was as astute as I knew she was, hence why I hired her, she would do the calculations, and a wise follow-up question would be about her subsequent paychecks and whether she would receive those on time. At that moment, it didn't look like it, but I was emotionally drained enough that I couldn't attempt to even have that part of the conversation with her. So here I was, a Top 30 Under 30 Mover and Shaker, yet indebted to her employee and trying to figure out whether I should let her go and run the risk of having dissatisfied clients due to a backlog of work, or keep her on, in hopes that cashflow would improve so that I could avoid more embarrassing confessions — because the truth was, not only did I feel bad about having her in that situation, but it was demoralizing for me.

That conversation would be the first of many instances of the same conversation for about four years.

Then there was the time I received a personal invitation to attend an exclusive social event because my accomplishments had caught the eye of some local movers and shakers. I respectfully declined, stating that I'd already committed to another event that evening. The truth was that I'd received a coveted local award, but my bank account was in overdraft and I didn't have gas money to get to the event, and certainly not for tips, parking, or other incidentals that come up when you are hobnobbing with movers and shakers. So, I declined, stayed home (although they thought I was busy), and looked at pictures of the evening later on, on Facebook.

There is also the fact that for about five years, I had to perfect, to the best of my abilities, my hairstyling and grooming abilities. Between forgoing my paycheck in favor of my staff getting paid, and keeping up with my own bills and responsibilities, I just did not have the money. Here I was, expected to compete with other millennials who somehow became rich overnight, maintained their fitness, and still remained flawless, and I couldn't even afford to go to the hair salon once a quarter. What do you do? If you're like me, you tap into the resourcefulness that led you down the path of entrepreneurship in the first place. I would watch YouTube videos, experiment on myself, and learn how to maintain my upkeep. To others, it was one more impressive skill that I had. To me, it was a matter of survival so that my self-esteem wouldn't completely tank.

I remember one year I had to take a full-time job as a teacher to get back on my feet, while maintaining our client base, managing staff, and keeping P.E.R.K. Consulting going. My days consisted of early morning P.E.R.K. administrative work, then going to school, lunch-times at my desk working on P.E.R.K., then finishing my classes, and ending the evening with a follow-up with my staff. 8–10-hour work days easily became 14-hour work days, with half spent as an employee, and the other half spent as an employer. Juggling those hats proved to be challenging for a while—especially when my entrepreneurs' ego kept trying to surface. What kept me humble was knowing that truthfully, half of my teacher's salary was being used to pay my staff, and that money was automatic, so I could at least sleep better that year. Additionally, for the first time, in some time, I could actually afford the simple things like going to the hairdresser and getting the occasional manicure.

While this was going on, there was no public announcement about my new lifestyle. To P.E.R.K. followers, it was business as usual. However, on the backend, I knew the embellishment and the great sacrifice that was going into making sure business continued as usual.

Now, are you sure you still want to go through with this? I thought so! Congratulations, you just got over the first hurdle, which is mindset.

Business Tip #1: Building From Within—Infrastructure Is Everything!

If you and I were sitting down for coffee, and I asked you what you believed was the single most important determining factor for success in business, what would you say? If you're like most people, you might respond that it's something along the lines of perseverance, determination, commitment, talent, or focus. What if I told you that while those things are important, they're not the most important factors? In fact, one of the biggest mistakes that I've seen entrepreneurs make is to rely on their skills and momentum for the success of their business. The hard truth is that those are two of the most dispensable parts of your business.

There are people who are just as talented as you, if not more, in your industry, and momentum is so fleeting and non-dependent on you that it's dangerous to rely on it. Even money is fluid and, by itself, does not determine the success of your business. There is only one thing that is singlehandedly more important to the success of your business. If not designed properly, you will get a false sense of momentum and your current positioning in the market, and without warning, can lose everything, if this one thing is destroyed.

The true key to a successful business lies in the strength of its infrastructure. I get it: most of us do not like creating systems. They're boring, tedious, and they take away from the time needed to actually do our business. If you're a clothes designer, you went into business to bring your designs and creativity to life. If you're a life coach, you want to help others improve their quality of life. I get it. You know the old adage about putting the cart before the horse? It's never been more applicable than in this context. Your cart is your thriving business—in a state that allows you to actually do what you love to do. Your horse is your infrastructure. The more robust it is, the more likely your business, in its ideal state, can go the distance.

So, what exactly is a business infrastructure? It is made of the basic facilities, structures, and services upon which the business is built. It is the system that makes everything run. It includes basic components like software and services, to more complex components like operational procedures. One of the primary benefits of creating these systems is automating your processes later on so that things can run like clockwork. For example, think about the transportation and tax systems in our country. As much as we hate it, we have to pay parking meters, tolls, and traffic violations to commute within our own communities. The idea and expectation is that this money does not get pocketed by our city officials, but is used to build and maintain our streets and neighborhoods. That is part of the economic infrastructure. It was a system that was thought of, fleshed out, executed, and is now an automated way that most cities collect money and fund needs. The same is true for your business. Creating an infrastructure allows for sustainability.

There are four areas of every business entity: operations, finances, capacity, and customer. If you think of your business as a house, those are the four walls. The operations wall is how your business runs—everything from the time you open your doors, until you close for the day, and what happens in between.

I've had the pleasure of consulting with hundreds of entrepreneurs, and the concern I hear most frequently is people feel like they're reactively going through the motions of business, rather than creating something that can be sustainable.

The ultimate test of whether your business has a sustainable infrastructure is to imagine walking away from it for a two-week vacation. What would happen to your operations? Would your team know what to do in your absence? Would your customers freak out? If the answer to the last two questions is yes, then you're currently lacking a sustainable infrastructure. Good systems depend on people, not just on a person.
A good infrastructure sees cashflow issues months and weeks ahead of time. The awkward conversations about late paychecks may occasionally happen, but by no means should be repeated to the point of becoming the norm. ☐

Lesson 2: Sorry, I Can't Hang Right Now. I'm in the Middle of Grinding (Social Health)

It was year two that I realized that my social life would never be the same. I was in the throes of everything I ever asked for—catching glimpses of financial independence, local and national recognition, independence to do work that was impactful and fulfilling, and consistent affirmation (evidenced by increasing word-of-mouth referrals) that my work was indeed good work. Each milestone only motivated and pushed me to accomplish more. Entrepreneurship is my drug of choice. The high of looking a challenge square in the face, strategizing on ways to conquer it, and then doing exactly that gives me the ultimate satisfaction. However, it wasn't long before I realized that all that good would cost me something.

My friend Lauryn and I have known each other for over 20 years, dating back to elementary school. To this day, she's still one of my best friends. Which is why when we both relocated, unbeknownst to one another, and reunited in our mid-20s in the DC area, our natural inclination was to see if we could pick up where we left things off. The newness of our reconnection was exciting—sharing college stories, taking in the DC nightlife as adults, and making plans for our respective futures. I supported her ambitions of starting her own haircare line (Purely Perfect Hair), and she supported my vision of putting my interest and experience with nonprofits to use by starting my own consulting practice. She supported it so much so that for the first year of P.E.R.K., she worked, pro bono, as our accountant.

I did good work—work that I was proud of, but work that was increasingly demanding of my time, resources, and attention. The better and more recognized P.E.R.K. became, the more personal investment it required. By the end of year two, weekly hangouts, not just with Lauryn but with all my friends, had turned into monthly hangouts. By year three—

my worst year in business to date—monthly hangouts had turned into infrequent "I'll see if I can make it" appointments only.

Part of the decline in social engagement, which I couldn't fully explain at the time, was my depleting financial resources. Forget discretionary income, I was lucky if I was able to get two paychecks in a row, as scheduled. This meant more fluid rainchecks, and less follow-through. As someone who deeply values relationships and people, this took a tremendous toll on me emotionally, especially because explaining my infrequent sightings would mean I'd then have to talk about the more embarrassing side of things—like how broke I was, even though one would never know by looking at my posts on Facebook, and the numerous awards I was receiving.

I remember one conversation I had with Lauryn. We were with a bunch of friends, and as usual, we were making plans for our next outing. Lauryn casually threw in there, "We'll see if Andrena can make it. You guys know she flakes sometimes." We all laughed about it, and I noticed that no one in the group disagreed with her. Even I didn't have a snarky comeback, because she was right. One of the things that I absolutely love about the friends—including Lauryn—that I have in my corner now is that most are absolutely honest. They're uncannily accommodating and kind, but they are brutally honest. Lauryn was right. I'd gone from an occasional flake, to having a reputation as a flake.

I thought about her comment for several months and analyze how I'd gotten to that place. There was the financial factor, which was embarrassing enough. There was a second factor, that wasn't so much embarrassing, as it was a seemingly natural part of settling into my new role. The other part of the social decline was the isolated nature of entrepreneurship that comes from the intense focus required, and the lack of (or fear of the lack of) empathy or understanding from those who are not entrepreneurs. Imagine checking into work at 9 am: you check your email, as usual. The first two things you see, after deleting what seems like hundreds of newsletters you're now subscribed to, so you can stay in the know, include one email from a disgruntled client, and another email about not being awarded a contract you'd been banking on. You let that news settle in, and you realize one of your staff is 30 minutes late.

You call to find out what's going on, and she tells you she's having some car issues and working on it right now. You sternly explain that it is a professional courtesy to call in when she is going to be late for work. She gives you some attitude, but agrees that she was wrong. You hang up to start a client project, and you notice that the client did not submit all of the information needed to start the work. You call her, and she's a bit of a talker, but you desperately need the contract, so you indulge her. What should have been a 15-minute telephone call easily turns into 30 minutes. It's now 10:30 am, and you're hungry. You have a lunch meeting scheduled at 12 pm with a potential partner, so you opt for bearing the discomfort (even though you skipped breakfast so that you could take care of a personal appointment at 8 am), because you really like the restaurant that you'll be going to. The lunch meeting goes well, but the partner is with a much larger organization, so your lunch date likely has to go through a few channels and superiors before the partnership can become official.

At 3 pm, you get back to the office, tired, but needing to start your client project in order to stay within the promised deadline. Your assistant asks about the meeting, and you provide some surface level answers, but divulging too much would blur the lines for professionalism. You keep the information in because at the end of the day, you are the final authority in the business. There is no sounding board—just yet. There are no forms to fill out. It's no one else's job to reprimand the employee who ended up being two hours late for work that day. As an entrepreneur, it all starts and ends with you, and this is what a typical day might look like.

As you can imagine, at the end of the day, you're either too tired to give anyone the play by play of your activities, or you're prevented from doing so because you don't want to be a burden, or you don't want to overshare your business and professional dealings, or you're not even sure where to begin—assuming you had someone to talk to. It becomes a repetitive cycle that can ultimately morph into a lifestyle—stress begets loneliness, which begets isolation, and isolation begets loneliness, which begets more stress.

The more I thought about this aspect of owning a business, the more I decided to look at how others were dealing with it. I was relieved to find that I was not alone. In fact, many serious entrepreneurs like Larry Page — co-founder of Google, Bill Gates — founder of Microsoft, and Elon Musk are notorious loners. We have an uncanny ability to lock ourselves away for days at a time in order to recuperate from the mental and physical exhaustion of our work, or to give our projects and vision our full attention. I've never been to this point, but there are some who even see social engagement as a distraction, and a dispensable part of life that can always be fixed later. Think about the popular quote from Jerry Rice: "Today I will do what others won't, so tomorrow I can do what others can't." Our culture honors social sacrifice. It's seen as necessary for success. I can relate, and I wholeheartedly agree that part of the price of success is sacrifice. However, the onus is on each of us to decide what price is too costly. For me, the barometer has become my mental health. When isolation starts to lead to depressive thoughts or angst, it's a warning that perhaps I've taken the sacrifice thing a bit too far. While it's still productive, I can set some alone time for myself. The trick, as with many things in entrepreneurship, is to ensure that I am honest with myself.

For me, early on, social sacrifice was necessary, but it was also misinformed and lacked maturity. I wholeheartedly believe that I would not own two businesses, and be the author of four books, if I'd spent most of my nights partying, hanging out, and socializing at every opportunity. However, after years of sustaining my business, I can look back and say that some of the sacrifice was not worth it. There are moments captured in photos that I regret not being a part of. There are relationships that were severed simply because I was not fully present. There were times that friends needed a listening ear, but I rejected the call because of a deadline. After watching thousands of dollars come and go, I've come to the conclusion that money is fluid, and your gift will always make way for you. However, time is finite, and sometimes, the better investment is in the relationship and the moment.

Business Tip #2: Be S.M.A.R.T.

Did you know that you can give 110% effort and fail miserably, even with a good goal? I've seen it more times than I can count. An eager entrepreneur has a brilliant idea, they align their resources, press the go button, and forge ahead, only to come back months later, disappointed that things are not working out. By the time they come to that realization, unfortunately, they've spent a lot of money, and invested energy and time that they will never get back. It is at that point that I explain that it is not the entrepreneur's fault. There was nothing wrong with their effort, resources, or idea. The reason for the apparent failure is that the goal was an inherently bad goal.

A good goal is not just noble in its intention, but it also a S.M.A.R.T. goal. It is specific, measurable, attainable, realistic, and timely. Ensuring that your goal meets these criteria increases the likelihood of success. It eliminates wasted time, and hones in on the best strategy for success.

Specific goals break down your general goals into manageable bite-size pieces, so that they are easier to achieve. A great example of this might be to increase your annual revenue. "Increase revenue in 2019" is a noble general goal. An even better goal is to "increase revenue in 2019 by identifying profit leaks and creating monthly marketing campaigns in order to obtain new clients." Using that example, it's easy to see how an entrepreneur can go from casting a wide net and taking a chance on what sticks, to identifying a specific strategy to achieve their goal.

Even that specific goal can be further developed as you think about other factors that will affect the outcome. By adding measurements and metrics like "increase revenue by 40% in 2019, by identifying profit leaks and creating monthly marketing campaigns in order to obtain new clients," the direction and initial action steps are even clearer.

The attainable and realistic factors in the S.M.A.R.T. formula are subjective factors that are determined by the individual's readiness to start working on their goals. For example, an entrepreneur who does not have a marketing budget needs to first raise the money or create a budget for marketing before embarking on the goal above. Without a budget, or the money for a robust campaign, attempting to increase revenue by creating marketing campaigns will prove futile. It seems obvious enough, but I have met and worked with many entrepreneurs who have failed to count the cost before they set their foot on the pavement.

The last piece of the formula is timeliness. This ensures that the person setting the goal has a sense of urgency and can fend off complacency when working toward their goal, no matter how difficult it may seem. It is easy to overlook this final piece, but it is just as critical as the others because it has two extremes: too much time allotted for the goal, and not enough time. When there is too much time, it is easy to fall into traps of procrastination and complacency. These are traps that force individuals to believe they have more time to do the work than they actually do. They lose their sense of urgency, which opens the door for others to leverage their ideas, or for a competitor to get to product launch before they do. The other extreme is not to give yourself enough time. By rushing toward the goal, entrepreneurs stand the risk of sabotaging by not properly assessing the risks and all of the factors necessary for success.

No goal is perfect, and neither is every process. However, the goal is not to guarantee success because, after all, there's value for the entrepreneur in trial and error and even failure. However, by ensuring that your goals are S.M.A.R.T., you set yourself up to experience the thrill of achievement that will become motivation for future success.

Lesson 3: Sometimes You Just Can't Fake It Until You Make It (Emotional Health)

I remember the first time I met him at a friend's house. He was incredibly smart, charismatic, and passionate—all the things I believed it took to own a successful business. As the night when on, I realized my original assumption was right. He did own a successful business, I learned from a friend who, as a good host, was doing introductions between all the people hanging out at her house. Staying true to my introverted side, at some point during the evening, I found a quiet corner just to get a few minutes of alone time. I pulled out my phone and did a quick search of the guy who had caught my interest—not in a romantic way, but in an intriguing "I'm fascinated by you" kind of way. This guy truly was the real deal. According to his digital footprint, he'd been in local and national media, he had thousands of followers on social media, and his business was a real business — systems, staff, and everything. I was impressed. Wary of coming across as weird, or romantically interested, I just secretly followed his business ventures after our initial meeting. Imagine my shock when, only a year after our meeting, I came across a press release that he was going out of business. It was a personal loss that I felt, because he'd secretly become a mentor of sorts. On a larger scale, I knew it was a huge loss to the community because his business did tremendous good in our local community — so much so, that his mission and philanthropic efforts had become a big part of his personal brand.

I read the contents of the press release, and I was dumbfounded. It went into great detail about his frustration with the lack of support (talk about guilt for not having the courage to actually let him know how much he was inspiring me), the personal financial difficulties he'd had to endure to actually start the business, the debt he'd accumulated for the sake of maintaining his business, and the toll all of it had taken on his mental health. He was tired, and he was closing shop and taking some time for himself. At 32 years-old, he was moving back in with his parents, and going to figure out his next move.

I only knew him through my friend, but I was sad for him. The sacrifice was familiar, and so was the weight of the pressure, the frustration, and the ultimate feeling of defeat. I was sad for him, but I was also, still, incredibly inspired by him. Not many of us are that honest. It reminded me of why I admired him—he embodied the entrepreneur spirit which often required leaving everything you had on the floor with sometimes only a conviction that you gave it your best effort.

While I admired him, I'd been going through my own woes. I remember the first time I came home to an eviction notice on my door. I'm not a stranger to financial hard times, but this time, it was different. Different because I was scheduled to be speaking at a local event for aspiring entrepreneurs later that week. The irony was enormous—I would be telling other people how to run a successful business, but my circumstances reflected that I was anything but successful. I was tasked with maintaining a happy front, while I had no idea if I would be homeless in 30 days. At this point, I believed I was in too deep to call it quits and get a traditional job. Even if I did, there was no way I could, with integrity, close my current client projects, give my staff notice, and get my first two paychecks in time to avoid eviction. I needed a miracle. Thankfully, that time, the miracle came. I can't say it came every single time, but it's come more times than not.

In the meantime, before the miracle came, I was dealing with the anxiety of possible impending homelessness, humiliation and fear of humiliation, deadlines that wouldn't take possible homelessness as an excuse, and the pressure of managing staff and making sure they were taken care of. It was an enormous weight to bear, and at the time, I didn't have a platform anywhere near the size of my friend's friend. I could only imagine that if he'd had as much to bear, it was no wonder he'd called it quits. There were few outlets for me at that time, as I committed to learning as I went. One of the outlets I had was my relationship at the time.

It had started as a good enough relationship, with the usual optimism and fearlessness of two young people in love. Ironically, it started shortly after I launched my business. There I was in my mid-20s, feeling empowered enough to launch a business, and loved enough to conquer any challenge that would come my way. I was in a great season in life. That is until it became an added stress. One of the things you won't learn in business school is that your emotional health is just as connected to your business performance as any technical skill that you will learn. What started as a good enough relationship soon turned toxic due to a mixture of our immaturity, my navigating uncharted territory "by myself," and a few other personal issues. When the stresses of my business coupled with the stresses from the relationship, I reached a breaking point. "I think we need a break," I told him. His response was, "I think you're right." That was the end of our relationship, which we'd told our family and loved ones was leading to marriage within a year's time. It was short, simple, and enough to send me down a spiral that lasted three solid years, with an extra year of residual impact. It affirmed that perhaps, he'd wanted out too. He, too, had had enough of the fighting, my mood swings, the instability that naturally comes with the ebbs and flow of entrepreneurship, and my overdependence on him. In hindsight, it was fair.

In that moment, all I felt was instant relief. Which I now see as further evidence of my poor emotional state. Most people grieve the loss of something valuable, yet I was relieved to take something else off my plate. The truth was that it wasn't just our relationship that was taking a toll on me. It was the mounting bills, the instability, the loneliness of not having the usual workplace comradery that I'd grown accustomed to, and the pressure of knowing that others were relying on me for their livelihood.

Another thing you won't learn about entrepreneurship in business school is that it is incumbent on you to get a hold of your emotions, triggers, and self-management skills, because at the extreme end, the stresses of entrepreneurship and seeming failure have led some to suicide, while at the lesser end, they may lead some to avoidable (and unavoidable) depressive breakdowns.

The bottom line is you get to a point where you realize that you simply cannot continue to fake it until you make it. It all gets to you. In those moments, it is not your business acumen, the number of followers you have, or even your five-star ratings that will save you. Salvation, in that moment, is depending on two things: your ability to separate yourself from your work, and how well you've developed your soft skills and your self-management skills, which are just as instrumental in your success as a business owner, wife, mother, husband, brother, or sister.

Business Tip #3: Marry the Mission. Date the Model

Just like with your personal life, one key to success in business is flexibility. When you first become an entrepreneur, most people you meet will throw a bunch of adages at you. Most of it is meant to be motivational, inspiring, and deep. For example, if you've already started your business, you may have already been told to "Hustle hard, relax later." It's said with good intentions, but the truth is, many of the adages have absolutely no significance to us until we are actually in the trenches of owning something. Many motivational quotes and adages that were thrown my way I honestly don't even remember. However, there is one that stuck with me, and frankly, it has saved my business several times over.

Marry the mission. Date the model. I learned the true meaning of this after my first year in business. The excitement and adrenaline had worn off, and the money I'd saved up for the initial capital had been depleted. I now faced "real" business issues, like cash flow and capacity building—issues that keep over 60% of businesses from making it past three years of operations. To marry the mission and date the model of your business means to be amenable to change, while maintaining your unique vision and solution (i.e. the product or service you offer).

Imagine this: for the past three years, several people have commented on how great you are at a certain skill set. Strangers notice it, your Facebook friends comment on it, and your close friends are now borderline annoying you that it's time to put your skills to use in a profitable way. After three years of confirmations, you finally decide to take action. You make an announcement via social media that you're finally taking a leap of faith to start that thing. Everyone is excited and relieved. Your friends are your initial customers, and you even have a few social media followers who actually go out to purchase your product or service. Month two comes around, and you notice a slight decline in transactions, but you figure you just need to keep the momentum going by advertising more. Month three comes around, and your sales are less than a quarter of what they were in month one, and frankly you're getting tired of constantly making a sales pitch. By month four, you're definitely discouraged. You start the introspection process, and then it hits you. You are having sales and cashflow issues because you realize this vision is going to cost a lot more than you originally anticipated, and your followers are now captivated by someone else who just made their launch announcement, offering the newest and biggest thing. The discouragement is now turning into frustration, resentment, and maybe even depression. You tell yourself it's no big deal because after all, entrepreneurs are problem solvers. This new side of the process is simply another type of challenge to work through. Except the problems increase at a much faster rate than you have the capacity to solve. You're stuck. Frustration turns to panic. Panic turns to fear. Fear turns to isolation, and for many of us, this is where the quitting begins.

So, how do you navigate this? The process for each of us is different, but it must start with remembering to marry your mission and date your model — and no, not in the infidelity sort of way. To marry your mission is to remember your why, and to maintain your covenant with that why. For some of us, we went into business to disrupt the industry. We were tired of seeing things done inefficiently, or annoyed that one or two people were monopolizing a sector, leaving no room for anyone else to play.

For others, there was a glaring need that one too many people complained about, yet no one was getting around to offering solutions. Then are others of us who started a business because we recognized our gifts and talents and saw them as a way to gain economic self-sufficiency. There are also those of us who simply went into business to walk in our purpose — we found a sweet spot where our gifts, opportunities, and experiences intersected, and decided to stay there and explore for as long as we could. Remembering this why is critical to your success. It is your mission. It lays the foundation for the story that your business will tell.

To date your model, on the other hand, is to make flexibility a bedrock of your business. It is your how. While your mission—the reason you went into business, and the need that your business solves—shouldn't change, the way your business does business had better change if it is to survive. The reality is that there are so many factors to your success as an entrepreneur that have absolutely nothing to do with you—there are industry trends, sales cycles, current events, economic upturns and downturns, and even your organization's current capacity. Being able to adjust to external influences (and some internal ones) will impact the likelihood of success.

I experienced this firsthand, with my reluctance to take advantage of the prevalence of social media. I'm a bit of an introvert, so in "real life," too much social is extremely draining. I imagine social media would be the same way. It seemed that on social media, the more pictures of yourself, and the more information you divulged about your life, the more popular you were. I considered the whole thing narcissistic and embarrassing, and I was not interested in any of it. The mistake I made in this instance was that I applied my personal preference and philosophy to my businesses, forgetting one of the first rules of business, which is to take personal feelings out of it and remember that business is business.

The awakening moment came when one of my friends, who has since gone on to become an Instagram celebrity-of-sorts said to me one day, "You need to do social media better. In fact, sometimes when I go to your page, I just want to exit out really quickly." I laughed, and thought how pathetic and shallow it was of her to assume that just because her pursuit was instafame, it should be everyone else's too. While she was earning followers, I was too busy earning real money. That is until I realized my aversion was actually costing me money—to the tune of $2,000 from one transaction alone. That may not be much to some people, but when you're building your business from the ground up, with no external funding, $2,000 may as well be $2 million.

The aha moment came when, in year three, we were so desperate for new clients, that we went along with the New Year's hype and invested $2,000 in radio advertising. I listened to the pitch from the advertising rep, and the data from the thick presentation folder only corroborated the success story she'd just told me with so much emotion and passion. I quickly went over our declining sales numbers, shook off the impending panic that I was sure would take over if things continued the way they were, and I signed on the dotted line. If we didn't see a return immediately, it meant that investing this money would result in me going without a paycheck for at least a month, but I would be able to recuperate the money once the phones started ringing from the advertising campaign. In the meantime, I could expect a few more late notices, and a few weeks of less-than-decent meals. However, it was a means to an end. The bigger picture, according to the marketing pitch, was that in no time, the phone would be ringing, my inbox would be flooded, and I would have more customers than I could manage. Of course, if this happened, in no time I would be able to give myself a raise and possibly even hire more people.

There's always optimism, but boy, was I wrong. Approximately three months went by before I finally accepted that I had thrown $2,000 down the drain. Forget an actual client—we didn't even get one inquiry from the campaign. In this case, ROI stood for Return on Ignorance, because it certainly did not stand for Return on Investment. This poor decision almost served as an omen because that year, which I now call the Year of Doom for P.E.R.K. Consulting, ended up being our worst year to date in business. Our revenue was less than 50% of the previous year, and as our revenue decreased, so did our capacity, as I had to terminate those who were left after those who had quit because they were tired of delays with their paychecks. I was back to square one, except with much more work now since we'd been around for a couple of years, and had active clients on our caseload.

The final quarter of that year demanded a revision of our strategies. Turns out my friend was right. With little money, and more time on my hands now, I decided to swallow my pride, and begin learning what others were now experts in because they had jumped on the social media bandwagon early enough.

The good news was that this wasn't a case that required us to scrap the whole business idea. After all, I did keep up the first part of the mantra—I married my mission. The reason I did business—my motivation, the solution I proffered, my distinguishing factor—never changed. It was the second part—the dating part—that needed help.

Think of it this way: your mission is the baseboard of your business. It provides the framework that connects your initial idea to the elements that allow your business to run successfully. The model is the paint you use to present that baseboard to your customers. Good business owners understand that the paint selection is not arbitrary, but it's a careful choice that considers trends, your current capacity, and the customer's preferences and position.

To put it another way, the mission is your why, while your model is your style. There's a reason you went into business in the first place. When you first take the leap, there's this incredible adrenaline rush that comes from seeing yourself actually manifest what's only been a vision in your mind for weeks, months, sometimes even years. There's also the rush and pride that comes from your friends, family, and followers being engaged with you, complimenting you, and urging you along. There's even a little bit of satisfaction that comes from knowing some people now hate on you and consider you a threat, simply because you had to courage to make a move, while some are still stuck in their ways, pining over shouldas wouldas couldas. That initial vision before everything else was added to the journey is your why. It's the thing you make a covenant with — to never forsake, to always keep at the forefront, and to commit to, in good times and bad.

Your style, on the other hand, should change. That style includes your marketing strategies, your price point, and sometimes even your culture. It's all still connected to the mission — the story that resonates with your audience — but those things allow you to stay relevant and top-of-mind.

As the Year of Doom came to an end, I was forced to make some difficult decisions, and the words of my friend came to mind: "You need to do social media better." True, my goal in life was not to become an Instagram celebrity, but to build a viable empire that existed for more than social media likes. We were building a company that had a previously effective offline strategy, and had become somewhat sustainable because we had loyal local customers, but with 50% less revenue, we gave the free option a real shot.

For six months, we decided that we would focus our efforts on establishing a digital presence. The results were incredible. What we couldn't even catch a glimpse of in 90 days with the radio station, we saw fully manifest within 30 days. Within just one quarter, our website visitors doubled and conversion rates increased by 80%, when compared to conversions in the same quarter in the Year of Doom. It was the miracle that took one year. By the following year, our revenue had increased, not only allowing us to recuperate from the previous disastrous year, but even exceeding every benchmark in our strategic plan. Had I not been open to changing the model, I am convinced that P.E.R.K. would've ceased to exist.

Your story may be different, but however change may look for a business owner to grow, it is important to remember to marry your mission and date your model.

Lesson 4: Where Did Those 30 lbs Come From? (Physical Health)

I stared at the scale again, mouthing the numbers. I knew I'd gained some weight. The extra-snug jeans that used to fit just right told me that. When that didn't do the trick, the candid picture posted on Instagram that showed a couple of chins definitely confirmed it. In that instance, there was a simple fix—untag myself from the photo. The camera always added 10lbs anyway, and besides, it was just a bad shot. At least that's what I told myself. However, as I looked down again at the scale, I knew the numbers did not lie. When my hustle resulted in hundreds of new followers in a matter of weeks, that was no lie. When I secured the contract that allowed me to hire my first real employee, that was also no lie. Numbers didn't lie then. Surely, they weren't lying now. This was not going to be a simple fix. I was the heaviest I'd ever been in my life, and it had been a long time coming. But how did this happen? Let me start from the beginning.

I've never been a thin girl. Truth be told, I've actually never wanted to be thin. Thanks to a good genetic pool, apparently from my paternal side, my proportions were (still are) what most girls strived for — wide hips, small(er) waist, and a proportional chest area. Whether I was a size 8 or a size 14, the proportions remained — sometimes just easier to see than other times.

When I got the idea for my first business, I was 25 years old, and a happy size 12. I had survived some disappointment after my plans for law school didn't pan out, and I had moved back to the East Coast after living in the desert — otherwise known as Ohio — for three years. (No offense to Ohioans — I mean desert as in the biblical wilderness, not desert as in deserted.) I'd gained some weight then, as I struggled to overcome the sadness and disappointment, but I was still healthy, vibrant, and a size 12.

While I was transitioning from making my business a side hustle to a full-time gig, I'd maintained my lifestyle. Emulating the successful entrepreneurs I saw on social media, I made it a point to work out a couple of days a week, my appetite was still consistent, and the quality of food I was eating was good. Year one saw minimal challenges. However, as time went on, my ability to maintain that lifestyle declined.

Perhaps it was the 10 hours I spent behind the computer, or the fact that I could no longer afford to buy a variety of foods, just what was cheapest. Perhaps it was the comfort eating from the stress of all of it. What if I failed again? There's nothing else to do, as I'd proudly told the world that I was now a business owner. Whatever the reason, those pounds crept up, and decided they'd find a comfortable place to rest...for three years. As my waist size increased, my skin deteriorated, I was constantly fatigued and too exhausted to hustle the way I had when I'd first started. I did not have as much discretionary income to shop, so when I outgrew clothes in my closet, I simply resorted to wearing the same things over and over again, resulting in the worst part of it all—the effect it had on my self-esteem.

The funny thing about unhealthy habits is that they don't seem to take a long time to be established, but they can take forever to rid yourself of. Desperate for change, but crippled by my lack of resources, I tried the crash diets, the rigorous exercises, and my last resort — total deprivation. Some methods were unsustainable. Some worked intermittently. Then I'd get comfortable again, and I would balloon. That is, until one day, it hit me — this was not just about vanity and weight gain, but my physical health was directly connected to my mental and emotional health. It was then that the game changed for me.

I remember teaching a course on S.M.A.R.T. goals. In it, I was empowering and helping others figure out how to be successful with their goals, yet I couldn't even successfully lose just 10 lbs. I determined then that there would be no more hypocrisy. I would teach what I believed, and follow my own advice. Operation Total Body Makeover would begin, and I would start with the core of it all, my heart and my mind.

Losing mental and emotional weight (baggage) meant finally dealing with my issues, starting with the imposter syndrome. With the breakdown of my earlier relationship, and the realization that it really hadn't done much to alleviate my stresses—in fact, it had only added to them—I had gone further into a cocoon of isolation, but fear that I would be found out—as broken, broke, stuck, insecure, and isolated.

What if they (my clients, followers, friends, and family) found out that some days I could barely get out of bed because I resented being awake, or that I was getting two hours of sleep because I could only get my work done in the silence of the night, when I didn't have to think for four people, instead of just me? What if my clients knew that many times I was making it up as I went along, and what I didn't know, I was making a mental note to look into later. What if everyone knew about the immense pressure that I placed on myself, believing I had three strikes against me—being a woman, black, and young? The thought of the exposure was unbearable. Then I found out that I was not alone. In fact, most founders and entrepreneurs struggle with imposter syndrome.

Imposter syndrome is a psychological pattern in which an individual doubts their accomplishments and has a continuous internalized fear of being exposed as a "fraud." You know you're not a fraud. Your intentions were noble and grand when you started, until you actually started. That's when you unearthed expectations, a new set of responsibilities, and dynamics that were never at play before. All of a sudden, your noble goals are in the rearview, and you feel like you're on the treadmill struggling just to keep up. That loss of control creates the doubts, and the fears, and some anxiety, and maybe even depression. The additional challenge is that at first, you think you can get it under control, but the more time that lapses, the more you realize the distance between your control and the expectations placed on you is greater. Hence, imposter syndrome.

I like to think that you're not really an entrepreneur until you've struggled with this. It means that others' expectations are simply a result of your perceived expertise and abilities. This can be founded in your reputation (so you do a good job of selling yourself, or other people rave about how great you really are), and/or your consistency. From the entrepreneur who is just starting out, to the greatest leaders like Sheryl Sandberg, Howard Schultz, and Maya Angelou, most of us will struggle with this at some point. No one is exempt. I certainly wasn't, and I was learning that the hard way as I realized that it played a huge role in my self-image and confidence at the time.

Step one in Operation Total Body Makeover was dealing with this. I actively sought help for my insecurities, and healing from the pain of my breakup. I regained my spiritual footing by going back to the basics of having that as my foundation in life. It was a process, but I found that the more baggage I was able to release, the more joy I gained, and I was able to see life with a clear lens again. Now, working out wasn't a task, but a necessary and at times even enjoyable outlet to rejuvenate my body, get some alone time, and regain control of my life. My confidence was no longer hinged on other people's opinions, but watching the numbers go down on the scale again brought me the private satisfaction of knowing I was practicing what I was preaching and reaching my goals.

Once I found a groove with new physical

habits, I happily incorporated new lifestyle choices, like becoming a vegan. Again, taking ownership of all aspects of my health, what started as a week-long personal challenge became a habit that accelerated my health goals. I quietly enjoyed the benefits for a few weeks, even losing 6 lbs in one week, until my first outing with friends to a restaurant required me to explain why my menu choices were drastically different from what my friends were used to seeing me order. As expected, some were shocked, but again, I had the quiet satisfaction of knowing that I was making bold moves that were not for public recognition or attention. As I had suspected all along, the weight loss, renewed mind, and improved confidence have intertwiningly led to the same levels—if not higher—of enthusiasm, creativity, and productivity I had in my first year of business.

Business Tip #4: Stick-to-it-ness— the Difference-maker

According to research from the Small Business Administration, only half of new businesses survive for the first five years, and only 35% are able to survive for 10 years. Even grimmer, Bloomberg research shows that 8 out of every 10 businesses fail within the first 19 months. Common reasons for business failure include leadership and management failure, weak value proposition, unprofitable business model, and poor financial management. The statistics are scary, but starting and running a successful business is not impossible. I have come to believe that what sets the successful apart from the unsuccessful is not luck, worth ethic, or even skill. It really boils down to the power of perseverance.

At the time of writing this chapter, I've successfully converted to an all-vegan lifestyle. Here's why I'm allowing myself a pat on the back: I grew up in a West African household where a meal was not complete without meat. I hail from a part of the world where for some people, a meal with meat is a luxury, and not to be taken for granted, but having access to it is a reminder of how fortunate you are. I have tried (unsuccessfully) to do similar fasts before and found it difficult to even go 24 hours without adding it to my diet. Yet, here I am, several months in, and not a bite of meat, or even a craving that can't be curbed, but with a mental clarity that I had yet to know. Same me, same moral compass, same culture, and same circumstances.

What made the difference this time around? Two words: intrinsic motivation. Defined as drive that is motivated by internal rewards and fueled by natural satisfaction, it is one of the biggest driving factors of success. For me, past attempts to change my diet and get healthy were motivated by external factors—looking good, fitting a specific dress, not being the biggest person in a photo, or even having a "summer body." There's nothing inherently wrong with those motivating factors, but as

I've learned, external factors are fleeting. Summer body is not enough motivation in November when the cold weather is a deterrent and bulky clothing allows me to stay warm and hidden. I needed something more, and I finally found the reason that is bigger than myself.

It started with week one. I lost 6 lbs, which was enough to motivate me for week two. The results from those two weeks—increased astuteness, productivity, better sleep, clearer skin, and slight improvements in my confidence were enough to motivate me to get through week three, which brought on the beginning of external signs of changes in my body. By week four, the new changes were becoming habits that were not fleeting, but a constant reminder that commitment and persistence did yield real changes. Get where we're going with this?

Like anything, your business requires a commitment driven by something bigger than yourself. What others won't tell you is that you'll have some seemingly brilliant ideas that just won't work. The timing may be off, the solution doesn't align with your audience's needs, you don't have the resources to really get things going, or you find that the idea needs to be fleshed out more. When it's an issue of timing, a good entrepreneur is able to align his resources and relaunch at a more appropriate time. When the idea needs to be re-directed, a good entrepreneur finds more appropriate solutions. Even the biggest companies in the world have gone through that. Taco Bell started as a hot dog stand. Wrigley's started as a soap maker, and Nintendo started as a playing card company. What happens when you notice a misalignment in your messaging, or that sales numbers are still down, or that your clients are going to a different company? This is where intrinsic motivation comes in. It starts with a commitment to legacy, flexibility, and solution-orientation—things that others may not notice on the outside, but things that keep you up at night, reallocating resources, planning three steps ahead, and reviewing data to ensure your success.

I have consulted with hundreds of organizations in my career. Some founders walk into my office and within minutes, I know they're going to make it. Some walk in, and by the end of the conversation, I have a pressing feeling that they'll be back at some point, most likely with a completely different idea from the initial one they came in with—not because they are serial entrepreneurs, but because they may fail and have to start all over. What makes the difference? Persistence. Persistence will take you places that your gifts, connections, and money can never take you. It is secretly admired, and outwardly evident. Want your business idea to succeed? Submit to the evolution process and commit to turning it into something that exists for more than just you, no matter how many tries it takes.

Lesson 5: You Mean It Was Never up to Me in the First Place? (Spiritual Health)

In the Year of Doom, I remember being curled up in the corner of my little office at 2 am. I'd slept there, again. I was exhausted by maintaining my pristine smile and leadership energy from 9 am–6 pm, then grinding in the evening by going to local bus stations to put up flyers, then trying the recommendations late at night for digital marketing. The month before, we'd made a total of $375 — as a firm. You read correctly: $375. What some make in minutes we'd made in a whole month, and it was supposed to pay our office rent, software subscriptions, payroll, and more. Of course, in an attempt to be a good leader, my needs were the first to be sacrificed. I'd tried everything. None of it was working. To say we were in a drought was an understatement. And I was pushing through it alone.

Finally, I'd crashed and burned. I had to ask for help. Like most entrepreneurs, it is contrary to my nature to give up, but there was no way I could go to bed for another day on a hungry stomach. So there I was, at a crossroads where I was watching it all slip away, but holding on for dear life on the one hand, and questioning the point of it all on the other hand. It took me a while, but I finally did ask for help, and surprise, surprise, there were people who were willing to help me. That's a story for another day.

Fast forward several months later, and I got a call from a prospective client I'd met nearly ten months prior. He needed some work done, and he needed it fast. As we spoke on the phone, I calculated all of our expenses, considered what was fair, so as not to undercharge (my previous tendency had been to undercharge without substantial consideration for our expenses), and gave him a quote. It was nearly twice what I would have previously charged. He agreed, and said he'd come in to sign the contract. He followed through. A few days later, another prospective client that I met through a networking opportunity called. Same deal — they needed a project completed, with the same urgency, and they were willing to pay nearly twice what I'd previously charged. In less than a week, without much trying, we'd secured two contracts that were going to put a significant dent in the debt we'd accumulated over the year. True, the money was budgeted and allotted out before it even hit our account, but at least I could sleep easier, knowing that I could at least keep one or two of my promises to "work things out." This was a critical juncture for us as I realized that while I had to take control of my business as a leader, there were things that were way beyond my control, and even on my best day, even I could not manipulate time into doing what I wanted it to do. My clients' resources, their aha moment of recognizing their need, their choice to use us as their consultant, my employees' flexibility and investment into their work, when our advertising would reach the ideal customer positioned to make a move right at the time of our need — these were all things beyond my control. Sure, I could spend a lot of money on advertising to increase the probability of success, but the radio station debacle proved that investment into marketing does not ensure success. I was face to face with the reality that there were forces at work that also influenced our bottom line and results.

My Christian faith has also been the biggest influence in the way I do life. Naturally, it also affects the way I do business. During the Year of Doom, watching things beyond my control crumble around me—and watching other things, also beyond my control, align in my favor—actually reaffirmed my faith and Christian foundation. That year, I took hold of Psalm 126:5-6 as a personal promise: "Those who sow with tears will reap with songs of joy. Those who go out weeping, carrying seed to sow, will return with songs of joy, carrying sheaves with them." For more than a year, I'd experienced the tears and weeping part, and I believed that these two new clients were signs of the beginning of the turnaround: the reaping and joy part.

I was right. Things continued like that for several months—intermittent but substantial projects from unlikely sources. The biggest turnaround came when a former colleague emailed me. I'd worked with her 13 years prior, when I was a student intern and she was staff. She'd been following my work with P.E.R.K. via our newsletter, and she asked if we did capacity building and leadership training. She had a project coming up, and she'd thought of me. I quickly jumped on the opportunity, prepared a proposal for her, and sent it off. I couldn't let on to how anxious I was, but this one project was likely to change everything for us — in fact, that one project alone was worth what we typically earned over four months (during our good seasons). She responded soon after, and just about guaranteed us the contract. It ended up changing the trajectory of P.E.R.K., and renewed my conviction that my success was just as dependent on God's favor as it was on my work ethic and skill. I'd failed miserably, and I'd lost a lot, but just like that, and without any intentional personal engagement for me, I'd been awarded a contract to do something that I likely would have done for free because I enjoy it so much.

Thinking about the whole exchange, I still marvel at the supernatural nature of how things transpired; how a colleague I hadn't seen or talked to in thirteen years would automatically trust me for such a substantial project, why she'd remember me of all the people she must have encountered during those years, and how I didn't have to do anything—no pitch, no lunch meetings, nothing—and how that money was enough to help us claw our way out again. The miracle was not only in those things, but through the whole process, I saw more glimpses of God's grace.

When I first submitted the proposal, I'd underbid out of fear of losing the opportunity. As I read through her emails, she'd made it clear that there was room in the budget for me to ask for slightly more. I took her hints, considered the reality of our situation, and asked for a few thousand more. It was granted. Just like that. We performed the project, which spanned three full days. In three days, we made what, in a good year, took nearly four months to make. This affirmed my faith that God is a master mathematician. The miracle continued because, a year later, she came back to us to perform the same work.

Every time I think about that situation, I still get emotional thinking about the sequence of events. For nearly 12 months, I'd put my foot to the pavement thinking that our cashflow, client recruitment, and retention would always be a direct reflection of the amount of work that I put in. I was wrong. The lesson here was about stewardship—seeing myself in my rightful position in the business as manager, not owner. After all, walking in my God-given purpose was still a huge part of my why and my intrinsic motivation.

There is a lot to be said for work ethic, because if you don't work hard, you simply cannot be entrusted to carry out a vision that God wants you to carry out. However, recognizing your limitedness in humility before God is probably the biggest key to success that I've come to realize. Deuteronomy 8:18 says it is God that gives us the ability to make wealth. All my months of sales calls, outreach, and canvassing, and lowering prices in desperation had failed, but desperate times call for desperate measures. It was not until, in humility, I declared a fast and committed to going to my church at 6/7 am every morning by myself to pray that I began to see changes in my business. Not just any changes, but supernatural, unmerited, favorable changes and solutions that had never even crossed my mind.

The one thing I tell entrepreneurs today, especially Christian entrepreneurs, is that if you're struggling in your business, go back to basics. For me, that looked like not taking my prayer time for granted, continuing to tithe and intentionally give, knowing that my giving is a seed that God honors. It also looked like posting print-outs of scripture references and God's promises on my desk and around my home so that I would always have a visual reminder that the enterprise was not mine. The results were unearthly.

After the contract with the university, it seemed we could do no wrong in business for several months. Our caseloads became full again, and workshop and training tickets began to sell. In fact, for months, there was not a day that went by that money did not come into our account. Where we used to wait until a certain week in the month to collect on invoices, I was waking up in the morning to notifications about payments. When I was tempted to brag about that, I was reminded that not too long prior, my best efforts had yielded minimal results. But in faith, my minimal efforts had yielded the best results. I share these things not to imply that God is some kind of magical genie, but to reiterate that sometimes all of the good business advice, a strong work ethic, and controlled factors may not be enough to guarantee your success. I've learned that more times than not, it takes divine intervention and answered prayers to remind me that there is someone much bigger than me who is also rooting for my success.

Business Tip #5: Cashflow Is King. Diversification Is His Queen

Poor cashflow management is among the top reasons for small business failure. All over the world, entrepreneurs are struggling with similar issues: minimal performance management structures that allow business owners to accurately anticipate challenges, lack of funding, and poor financial management systems. What if I told you that the money will come, if you create systems that are conducive to bringing it in? Let's start with mindset.

The average millionaire has seven streams of income. One or two of those may be active streams, like a full-time job or owning and managing a business, but the remaining are considered side hustles or passive income. The key here is diversification — understanding that it takes more than one stream to ensure cashflow fluidity.

It's always amazed me that everyone wants to be the next Warren Buffett or Steve Jobs, but overlooks foundational strategies like diversification of income. As it is with individuals, so it is with your business. To rely on one or two streams of revenue exclusively is economic suicide. Good business owners understand that there are challenges external to the business that impact productivity, sales, and conversion. For example, if you're a service provider like a nonprofit consultant, a grant cycle has a tremendous impact on the organization's capability to retain your services. That has nothing to do with your competency, business development strategies or fit, or the organization. Or, let's say you are in a product-based arena like retail. Similarly, there are challenges that impact your sales that have nothing to do with you, like whether your product is in-season, shipping and tax rates, or whether your customers have discretionary income for that product at that time.

The truth is, it is not your customer's job to be readily available to purchase. It is your job to appeal to several customers so that at any given time, you are successfully engaging as many as you can. For the nonprofit consultant, additional streams of revenue may include writing a book or creating a workbook that she can sell on her website passively as an additional stream of income. She may also want to consider teaching live classes in her local community for a fee or creating a fee-based webinar that she can conduct from the comfort of her home. These additional options will ensure that even when there is a lull with her signature services, there is still revenue coming in to sustain her business.

Think about it this way: if big box stores have to default to bankruptcy after seasons of scarcity, how much more do fledgling entrepreneurs have to grind daily for each penny and customer to stay afloat? To get a better handle on this, I recommend business owners complete the systems management analysis found at the end of this book. The finances quadrant allows business owners to create a financial system founded in diversification as a core value. By doing so, you put your business in a better position to not only survive, but to thrive. No one desires it, and it is within reason to panic, but if there is a season of scarceness, a good financial and cashflow system can continue even if the passive streams are carrying the business for a while, while the larger issues are fixed. Entrepreneurship is not for the faint of heart. It demands creativity, flexibility, persistence, and innovation. I believe that you picked up this book because you have all of those qualities. They're what sets the successful and unsuccessful apart. Now that you have received five tips for success, understand and internalize that you can be one of those who succeeds and lives to tell about it. The world needs your vision, your story, your product, and your service!

It Gets Getter

Entrepreneurship is hard work. Anyone who has ever attempted to take the leap can attest to that. However, most will also attest that it is worth it. The heartbreaks and disappointments that I've experienced have been matched, at some point, with incredible satisfaction and fulfillment. Like when I first resigned from my full-time job, only to later be given a more lucrative offer as a training professional with the same organization. With this new offer, I was able to work on my own terms earning in days what I used to earn per year.

Then there are the countless moments that I meet with a client who, with great passion, explains what they believe to be their life's purpose. They give me the background of how they've saved money and overcome great obstacles, and they're moved with compassion to start a nonprofit. They conclude with how they're trusting me to help bring their vision to life. They take my word that I could help them get their idea off the ground. Years later, these same clients are providing services for thousands of people internationally. Others are working diligently locally to change the community. Those are the stories that I cannot even put monetary value on. I take pride in knowing I am a part of their story.

A few years ago, a young lady sent me a private Facebook message. She was angry and resented me because my social media profiles made it seem I had "a perfect life." She was annoyed because she'd unsuccessfully tried starting several businesses, and it seemed mine was coming together seamlessly. My first response to her message was anger. She'd crossed the line, and she didn't know me well enough to send me such a hateful message. Anger was succeeded by sadness. She really didn't know that yes, the glamour and the highs were real, but so were disappointments, brokenness, fatigue, loss and loneliness that only those closest to me were privy to. I wrote this book to tell that part of the story — the part that gets lost in Instalives and press releases.

Entrepreneurship is work, but I've also come to believe it's worth it. Your hard work is worth it and so is your commitment to walk in purpose, and the legacy that you'll leave behind. No matter how difficult it gets, understand that your success starts and ends with that belief that you can make it.

Bonus: The #TuesdayTip Series

If you follow me on social media, you know that from time to time, I try to put up my unedited thoughts about business, entrepreneurship, and life in general through my #TuesdayTip and Dear #entrepreneur series. Many of you responded well to the series, so here are a few of my favorites. Are there one or two that really stand out to you? Feel free to use them as your own personal weekly motivation tools. And please share with me on Twitter! Here are the tips:

1. Do-overs are allowed. It's your vision and your life. You get to make the rules.
2. Your gift will make room for you. Don't worry about what everyone else is doing. Be a good steward of your gift.
3. Be consistent. You don't need a whole bunch of different ideas. Be consistent and work through the one that will change others' lives.
4. Failure is not final. It's a setup for a great comeback.

5. You don't need a lot of people to make the dream work. Invest in the few that get it and cultivate those relationships.

6. You're built for this. Just a reminder that you will make it.

7. The timing of a thing is sometimes just as important—if not more so—than the thing itself. If you just can't wait for it, carefully consider whether you're actually really ready for it.

8. Be likable—have a good attitude, be kind, be fair, be humble. You can have a mediocre product and people will buy from you, if they like you. Alternatively, you can have a great product, and people will still not buy from you, if they don't like you.

9. Familiarity breeds contempt. Maintain healthy boundaries. Maintain peace.

10. What other people assume about you is none of your business. Don't stoop. Don't engage. Keep it moving. Guaranteed, they'll find something else to assume.

11. All the money, recognition, and accolades in the world mean nothing if there's no peace and no one around to share it all with. Go as hard with family time, rest, and balance as you do with your projects and work.

12. Everything does not need to be on social media. The person you connected with 10 years ago but haven't talked to since, and the person who follows you, but low-key doesn't really care for you, do not deserve the same access to your life as your best friend. Be selective and keep some accomplishments, the fight with the boo, your bank account, your list of haters, some hard times, some meals, and some business moves sacred and private. It's ok. Don't wait for next year. Start now. Regain. Your. Sanity.

13. Promotion without good character quickly turns to misery. Pray for the grace (and strive) to obtain both.

14. When you're building your vision, there will be moments when you're outsmarted, outdone, and even outworked, but commit to never letting yourself be outlearned.

15. You can view your past experience as a failure, or as a practice round. The effectiveness of your next move will be determined by that perspective.

16. Self-reflection is a much kinder teacher than regret is. Prioritize yourself by making a habit of it.

17. Being underestimated is one of the biggest blessings you can ever have. Don't be mad. Don't be proud. Don't despise it. Use the surprise element, and work it to your advantage.

18. Want influence? Be quiet. The most powerful person in the room is rarely ever the loudest. It's usually the person practicing the art of observation.

19. Guard your heart, mind, and time. Those three things will determine the health of everything else in your life.

20. Be mindful of people who always have to be one up on you. Be careful not to become that person.

21. Name your price. Freedom and purpose will cost you something, but so will comfort and regret. Decide which is too expensive. Commit, then give yourself permission to go through the process.

22. Don't waste time defending yourself to people who don't need a reason to dislike you. Treat your time and energy like the commodities they are.

23. Consistency opens doors that skills, connections, and external resources cannot. It's ok to go at your own pace, but by all means be consistent.

24. Some call it instinct. Others call it intuition. Whatever you call it, always trust the Spirit of God within you. If it smells and looks funny, 9 times out of 10 it is absolutely funny. Discernment is your God-given superpower. Pray for it and use it well.

25. There are people who will make their way into the fold for the sole purpose of finding out how and why you do things. Sometimes it's to sabotage, or so they can leverage their association. Other times it's so they can figure out how they can do it too. You can't prove their intentions. You just know it doesn't feel right. Pray for discernment (not paranoia, or baggage from past hurt or betrayal), trust God, commit to decisions, and keep it moving. You have that feeling for a reason.

Business Development Templates

SWOT Analysis

A SWOT analysis is a strategic planning technique that can be used to identify strengths, weaknesses, opportunities, and threats related to your business idea or project. The "S" and "W" are part of what is considered an internal environment assessment because they look at factors that can be controlled and are within the organization. The "O" and the "T" are part of what's known as an external environment assessment because they are outside of the organization, but just as critical to success.

Strengths
(List here anything you can think of that makes your organization amazing! What can you rely on to deliver your services? This can be anything from a known strength of the business owner or staff, or based on positive feedback from customers.)

Weaknesses
(What isn't quite the way it should be yet? What is missing? This can be based on observations, experiences, or feedback from clients and customers.)

Opportunities
(List here any potential opportunities to really push your organization forward that you have not yet taken advantage of. This can be a current event, a relevant trending topic, or even a misstep from a competitor that you can leverage.)

Threats
(List here anything that might get in the way of you achieving your goals—such as funding you aren't sure of yet, relationships that might break down, or regulatory factors.)

Systems Management Template

There are four major areas of every entity — finances, operations, capacity, and customer. If your business were a building, these would be the four walls. As a business owner, it is your job to create systems that will allow each area to stand on its own, while upholding the whole entity. To create your systems, start with the questions in each quadrant.

Finances
(How does your business earn and spend money? Are there several streams of revenue? If so, identify the logistics of each stream. If not, think about what other ways you can use your current resources to introduce a new product line or service to your customer.)

Operations
(How does the business run? Who is in charge of which aspect of the business? Are there documented systems in place that others can refer to if you are not around? Use this space to outline your operational goals and procedures.)

Capacity
(Do you have the right people in place? The capacity quadrant looks at human resources and equipment necessary to operate at an optimal level. Use this quadrant to identify whether there is a need to outsource work or parts of managing the system.)

Customer
(Who is your ideal customer? Start by creating a customer profile that includes demographic information and consumer behavior of your ideal customer. If you have several products or services, identify the ideal customer for each offering. Your marketing strategy and price point, among other things, will be directly influenced by your

ideal customer's profile.)

About the Author

Andrena Sawyer is the founder and president of P.E.R.K. Consulting, an advisory firm for small to mid-sized nonprofits and businesses, and the Founder of the Minority Christian Women Entrepreneurs Network (MCWEN).

Originally from Freetown, Sierra Leone, she and her family moved to the United States when she was nine years old due to the Sierra

Leonean civil war. She now credits her family's move for her interest in human triumph and perseverance.

For her work with nonprofits and small businesses, she has been honored among The Black Business Review's 40 Under 40, the International Alliance for Women World of Difference 100 Award, the Women Owned Small Business Award by the Associated Black Charities, and Hope for Africa Leadership in Community Development Award.
In addition to her work with P.E.R.K. Consulting, she is also the author of The Other Side of Assertiveness, Ponder It In Her Heart, and The Long Way Home.
To learn more about her, connect with her on Instagram and Twitter @Andrena_Sawyer.

Other Books By Andrena Sawyer

Fiction

The Long Way Home

What happens when Mr. Wrong turns out to be Mr. Right? Alonna Jones is no stranger to disappointments and heartbreaks. Struggling to deal with a devastating breakup and the lingering effects of bad decisions, she decides to move back east. As the secrets of her past continue to haunt her, she vows that she will never allow another man to get close to her heart again. On her journey back to the place she's always called home, Alonna learns that home is not only where the heart is, but also where redemption and healing can take place.

Ponder It In Her Heart

What happens when someone threatens to destroy the life you've worked hard to build? Beautiful and successful Nicole Sanchez is months away from marrying her best friend, but she will tell anyone who will listen that the life she's built was not handed to her on a silver platter. Despite being raised by an abusive mother and having an absentee father, it seems things have finally turned around for her. But just as life is coming together, a visitor from the past resurfaces. His appearance begins a domino effect that threatens everything she's worked hard for. With the layers falling apart, will she allow fate to take its course, or can she find the strength to keep fighting for what was promised to her? Join Nicole on her journey of strength and restoration.

This is a stand-alone sequel to The Long Way Home

Nonfiction

The Other Side of Assertiveness

Assertiveness is defined as "Characterized by bold or confident behavior," and, "Having a strong or distinctive flavor or aroma." For the assertive woman, this definition is by far one of the highest compliments. Many books have been written about how women can become more assertive. Women grow up hearing from parents, teachers, coaches and mentors about the importance of being assertive. However, what no one ever explains is that assertiveness comes with a price and it is easily mismanaged and misunderstood. Within the pages of this short eBook are some hard-hitting, humorous, and even hopeful lessons about the sometimes daunting effect of being an assertive woman in this day and age.

All available for purchase on Amazon!

Learn more about creating a sustainable business at www.perkconsulting.net

www.ingramcontent.com/pod-product-compliance
Lightning Source LLC
Chambersburg PA
CBHW071039240526
45469CB00006BD/2274